Sanjeev Kapoor's
KHAZANA

Mango Masti

In association with Alyona Kapoor

Popular Prakashan
www.popularprakashan.com

Published by
POPULAR PRAKASHAN PVT. LTD.
301, Mahalaxmi Chambers
22, Bhulabhai Desai Road
Mumbai - 400 026
for KHANA KHAZANA PUBLICATIONS PVT. LTD.

First Published 2010
Third Reprint March 2012

(4283)
ISBN: 978-81-7991-535-6

Design: FourPlus Advertising Pvt. Ltd.

PRINTED IN INDIA
by Saurabh Printers Pvt. Ltd.
A-16, Sector 4, Noida

AUTHOR'S NOTE

When summer comes around, it brings searing heat and sticky humidity. Strangely though, it is welcomed with open arms by everyone in India. That's because summertime is mango season!

In March, fresh green keri or unripe mangoes first make their appearance and are eagerly snapped up for making pickles and chutneys. By April and May, it is time to feast on the golden sweetness of the Alphonso or 'hapus' which is one of the most sought-after varieties of mango. Besides the Alphonso, there is the payri, the dussehri, langra, kesar, neelam, banganapalli – and these are just a few of the one thousand kinds of this heavenly fruit available all over the world!

The mango is not only one of the most versatile of fruits – it can be pickled, chutney-ed, made into jams, delicious milkshakes, ice creams and juices, added to curries and turned into the fluffiest of desserts – it can also be classified as a 'superfruit'. A superfruit is one which besides being appealing to look at and tasty, is also chock-full of nutrients and antioxidants that help fight disease.

India grows half the world's total crop of mangoes (averaging 10 million tonnes annually), which is no surprise considering that the fruit is believed to have originated here nearly 4000 years ago.

'Mango Masti' is my collection of delicious recipes with your favourite fruit. There are pickles galore including Gor Keri, Andhra Avakkai and Mango Thokku. Enjoy traditional thirst-quenchers like Aam ka Panna and the exotic Mango Margarita. Whip up a silky Mango Smoothie or a healthy Mango Lassi. Go on to Kairi Murgh and Aamras ke Malai Aloo served with sour and sweet accompaniments like Ras no Fajeto. For a sweet ending try the Mango Cheesecake or the Singaporean Mango Jelly.

All recipes serve four and are set out in easy-to-follow steps.

So go ahead and have some Mango Masti!

Happy Cooking!

CONTENTS

KADHI AND RICE

PICKLES, CHUTNEYS AND JAMS

DESSERTS

ANNEXURE

MANGO SMOOTHIE

Ingredients

3 large ripe mangoes, peeled and chopped

1 medium ripe mango, cut into ½-inch cubes, to garnish

3 cups chilled milk

6 tablespoons chilled yogurt

8 tablespoons sugar

10-12 ice cubes, crushed

Method

1 Place the chopped mangoes in the freezer for a while.

2 Process together the chilled mangoes, milk, yogurt, sugar and crushed ice cubes in a blender.

3 Carefully pour the mixture into individual glasses.

4 Serve chilled, decorated with mango cubes.

AAM KA AABSHOLA

Ingredients

- 500 grams unripe green mangoes
- 3-4 sprigs fresh mint
- 1 lemon
- ½ cup powdered sugar
- salt to taste
- rock salt to taste
- 4-5 black peppercorns, crushed
- 1 teaspoon roasted cumin powder
- chilled club soda

Method

1 Chill the serving glasses in a refrigerator. Wash, boil and peel the mangoes and extract the pulp.

2 Reserve a few mint leaves for garnishing and purée the rest. Cut the lemons into round slices.

3 Combine the mango pulp, sugar, salt, rock salt and two cups of water in a pan.

4 Cook over high heat for one minute. Add the crushed peppercorns, roasted cumin powder and puréed mint leaves. Stir and cook for two to three minutes.

5 Remove from heat and pass the mixture through a sieve. Cool.

6 Fill a saucer with table salt. Rub a slice of lemon along the rims of the chilled glasses and dip the rims in the salt.

7 Pour some of the mango mixture into the glasses. Top up with club soda.

8 Garnish with mint leaves and a slice of lemon and serve chilled.

Note: Unripe green mango contains loads of vitamin C, much more than the ripe fruit. As a summer drink, aam ka aabshola is unrivalled as it prevents ailments caused by heat. The name, literally 'firewater', has come from the Urdu áab or water and shola or fire, since it is made with a large dash of pepper.

MANGO-ORANGE PUNCH

Ingredients

- 2 cups mango juice
- 2 cups orange juice
- 4 tablespoons rose syrup
- 4 scoops vanilla ice cream
- 1 cup ice cubes

Method

1 Pour one tablespoon of rose syrup into each glass and swirl to form a design. Place the glasses in a refrigerator to chill.

2 Process the orange juice, mango juice and vanilla ice cream with the ice cubes in a blender till smooth.

3 Pour the prepared punch into the rose syrup-lined glasses and serve immediately.

Note: The word 'punch' derives from the Hindi word 'paanch' because it originally contained five ingredients - alcohol, water, sugar, lemon and tea or spices. The drink was introduced to Europe in the 1800's by the sailors and officers of the English East India Company returning from India. Today it stands for a variety of mixed fresh fruit drinks, which may or may not contain alcohol.

AAM KA PANNA

Ingredients

1	large unripe green mango
1	teaspoon cumin powder
4-5	black peppercorns, crushed
	black salt to taste
	a small pinch of asafoetida
½	cup sugar

Method

1 Wash and boil the mango. Let it cool. Peel, mash and strain the pulp.

2 Add cumin powder, crushed black peppercorns, black salt, asafoetida and sugar. Mix well till the sugar is dissolved.

3 Divide the mixture into four tall glasses and fill it up with chilled water. Stir well and serve.

MELON AND MANGO SMOOTHIE

Ingredients

1 medium ripe musk melon

2 ripe Alphonso mangoes

2 tablespoons strawberry crush

1 cup crushed ice

Method

1 Cut the melon into wedges, peel and remove seeds. Chop half a wedge into half-inch cubes. Chop the remaining melon into one-inch cubes.

2 Place in a freezer for an hour. Peel the mangoes and chop one slice into half-inch cubes. Chop the remaining mango into one-inch cubes. Place in a freezer for one hour.

3 Place the large cubes of melon and mango in a blender with the strawberry crush and one cup of crushed ice. Process till smooth and frothy. Pour into individual glasses and serve, topped with the smaller melon and mango cubes.

Note: Smoothies are an American invention and made their first appearance in California in the 1970s. They were drinks made entirely of fruit, fruit juice and ice, initially called 'fruit slush'. The slush became a smoothie when chilled milk was added! They are regarded as health drinks because of the presence of fresh fruits.

TROPICAL FRUIT AND NUT SMOOTHIE

Ingredients

2 ripe mangoes

1 apple

2 bananas

85 grams golden raisins

crushed ice

12-16 pistachios, chopped

Method

1 Peel and chop the mangoes. Peel and core the apple and cut into slices. Peel and slice the bananas. Place the fruit in a freezer till frozen.

2 Blend the frozen mangoes, apple and bananas with golden raisins and crushed ice in a blender. Pour into individual stemmed glasses.

3 Serve chilled, garnished with chopped pistachios.

MANGO MARGARITA

Ingredients

2 cups + 2 tablespoons of mango drink (bottle/carton)

a few saffron threads

8 tablespoons sugar

2 cups chilled club soda

4 tablespoons ripe mango cubes

Method

1 Soak the saffron in two tablespoons of mango drink.

2 Place the sugar in a pan and heat till it caramelises. Leave to cool.

3 Dip the rims of margarita glasses into the caramelised sugar.

4 Divide the mango drink equally between the four glasses and top up with club soda.

5 Swirl the saffron over and garnish with mango cubes. Serve immediately.

MANGO AND BANANA MILK SHAKE WITH MIXED FRUIT

Ingredients

- 1 small ripe mango
- 2 medium bananas
- 4 cups skimmed milk, chilled
- 2 tablespoons honey
- 1 cup ice cubes
- 8 grapes, quartered
- ¼ cup pomegranate kernels

Method

1. Peel and chop the mango and bananas. Place the pieces in a smoothie maker. Add half the chilled skimmed milk and process.
2. Add the honey and the remaining milk and process again.
3. Add the ice and process till it gets crushed.
4. Place the grapes in stemmed glasses and pour the milk shake over.
5. Sprinkle the pomegranate kernels and serve immediately.

AAMRAS WITH KESAR

Ingredients

1 kilogram ripe mangoes

¼ teaspoon saffron threads, roasted and crushed

1 cup sugar, powdered

2½ cups milk, chilled

Method

1. Remove the pulp from the mangoes. Pass through a piece of muslin.
2. Add the powdered sugar and the chilled milk.
3. Stir in the saffron. Serve chilled.

Note: Saffron is the most expensive spice known. The spice comes from the dried stigma of the crocus flower. Around 150 flowers are required to produce a gram of saffron threads!

MANGO LASSI

Ingredients

1	cup mango pulp
3	cups yogurt
¼	cup sugar
	crushed ice
¼	cup Chocolate Sauce (page 94)
15-20	pistachios, blanched and slivered

Method

1 Process the mango pulp and sugar in a blender. Add the yogurt and process again.

2 Add the crushed ice and process to a smooth mixture.

3 Pour the chocolate sauce into a squeezy bottle. Squeeze the sauce in a striped design along the inner sides of serving glasses. Pour the *lassi* into the glasses.

4 Garnish with some more chocolate sauce, and top with pistachio slivers.

5 Serve chilled.

MANGO AND PINEAPPLE SALAD

Ingredients

- 2 medium ripe mangoes, peeled and cut into ½-inch cubes
- ⅓ small pineapple, cut into ½-inch cubes
- ½ small head of lettuce, torn into bite-size pieces
- rock salt to taste
- 1½ teaspoons *chaat masala*
- ¼ teaspoon lemon juice
- 2-3 black peppercorns, crushed

Method

1. Place the mangoes, pineapple and lettuce in a large bowl.
2. Add the rock salt, *chaat masala* and lemon juice and toss well to mix.
3. Sprinkle the crushed peppercorns over the salad and serve immediately.

MANGO SALAD

Ingredients

1 large unripe green mango

1 large head of lettuce

1 cup chopped fresh coriander

1 fresh red chilli, seeded and chopped

2 shallots, chopped

2 tablespoons lemon juice

1 tablespoon light soy sauce

salt to taste

Method

1 Peel the mango and cut into long strips. Soak in iced water for ten minutes. Drain.

2 Line a large salad bowl with the lettuce leaves.

3 Combine the red chilli, shallots, lemon juice and soy sauce in a small bowl.

4 Mix the mango with the dressing and add the fresh coriander. Add salt to taste.

5 Transfer the salad to the bowl. Serve immediately.

INDIAN SALAD WITH MANGO DRESSING

Ingredients

- 3 tinned pineapple slices, drained and cut into 1-inch cubes
- 1 medium unpeeled apple, cut into 1-inch cubes
- 1 banana, peeled and cut into 1-inch cubes
- 1 large tomato, seeded and quartered
- 1 medium green capsicum, cut into 1-inch cubes
- 1 orange, separated into segments

Mango dressing

- ½ cup fresh ripe mango pulp
- ½ cup thick yogurt, whisked
- 1 tablespoon lemon juice
- 1 tablespoon cream
- salt to taste
- red chilli powder to taste

Method

1 Peel the mango and cut into long strips. Soak in iced water for ten minutes. Drain.

2 Line a large salad bowl with the lettuce leaves.

3 Combine the red chilli, shallots, lemon juice and soy sauce in a small bowl.

4 Mix the mango with the dressing and add the fresh coriander. Add salt to taste.

5 Transfer the salad to the bowl. Serve immediately.

CHEF'S TIP

To keep the apple and banana cubes from turning brown, rub them with a slice of lemon.

MANGO SASAM

Ingredients

- 3 medium ripe mangoes
- ¼ cup green grapes
- ¾ cup grated coconut
- 2 Bedgi red chillies, seeded and roasted
- ¼ teaspoon mustard seeds
- 1 teaspoon tamarind pulp
- 2 tablespoons grated jaggery
- salt to taste

Method

1 Peel the mangoes, remove the seeds and cut into one-inch cubes.

2 Grind together the coconut, red chillies, mustard seeds and tamarind pulp with one-fourth cup of water into a coarse paste. Add the jaggery and process once again.

3 Place the mango cubes and grapes in a bowl. Add the salt and the ground *masala*. Mix well and serve cold.

Note: When mangoes are not in season you can make the *sasam* with other fruits like ripe banana, orange, pineapple, apple etc.

CORIANDER PRAWNS WITH MANGO SALAD

Ingredients

¾ cup small prawns, peeled and deveined

½ cup Green Chutney (see below)

1 small unripe green mango, peeled and cut into thin strips

2 medium tomatoes

1 teaspoon mustard paste

salt to taste

4-5 tablespoons sugar

½ teaspoon black peppercorns, crushed

1 teaspoon lemon juice

4-5 iceberg lettuce leaves, placed in iced water

Method

1. Halve the tomatoes, remove the seeds and cut into strips.
2. Marinate the prawns in the green chutney for about fifteen minutes.
3. Heat a *tawa* and cook the prawns till done.

4 Mix together the raw mango strips, tomato strips, mustard paste, salt, sugar, crushed peppercorns, lemon juice and one tablespoon of water.

5 Add the grilled prawns and toss. Serve on a bed of iceberg lettuce.

Note: Coriander is also known as Chinese parsley and cilantro. All parts of the plant are edible including the roots!

GREEN CHUTNEY

Grind together 1 cup fresh coriander leaves, ½ cup fresh mint leaves, 2-3 green chillies, black salt to taste, ¼ teaspoon sugar and 1 tablespoon lemon juice to a smooth paste using a little water if required.

FISH AND GREEN MANGO CURRY

Ingredients

8 one-inch thick slices of king fish

2 medium unripe green mangoes, peeled, seeded and sliced

2 tablespoons lemon juice

Salt to taste

1 teaspoon turmeric powder

6 tablespoons oil

1 cup + 2 tablespoons grated coconut

1 medium onion, chopped

1 tablespoon red chilli powder

½ teaspoon mustard seeds

4 green chillies, slit

1 tablespoon coriander powder

10-12 curry leaves

1½ tablespoons rice flour

1 tablespoon tamarind pulp

2 tablespoons chopped fresh coriander

Method

1 Marinate the fish in a mixture of the lemon juice, salt and half a teaspoon of turmeric powder for about fifteen minutes.

2 Heat two tablespoons of oil in a pan and shallow-fry the fish till half done. Drain and set aside.

3 Soak one cup of grated coconut in one cup of warm water for three to four

minutes. Grind and squeeze to extract the milk.

4 Heat three tablespoons oil in another pan. Add the onion and sauté till soft. Add half the remaining turmeric powder, half the chilli powder, remaining coconut and salt, and sauté for two to three minutes. Add two cups of water and let the curry simmer for five minutes.

5 Add the remaining oil to the pan in which the fish pieces were fried. Add the mustard seeds, green chillies, coriander powder, remaining chillli powder, curry leaves, remaining turmeric powder, mango slices and sauté.

6 Strain the onion curry into the mixture, pressing well to extract all the flavours. Add the fried fish. Mix the rice flour with quarter cup of water to make a smooth paste and add to the curry. Cook stirring continuously till the curry thickens.

8 Add the coconut milk and stir. Add the tamarind pulp and bring the gravy to a boil. Remove from heat and garnish with the fresh coriander.

9 Serve hot with steamed rice.

MANGO GOSHT

Ingredients

- ½ cup peeled unripe green mango pieces
- 600 grams boneless lamb or mutton
- ¾ cup yogurt
- 1 teaspoon dried mango powder
- 1 teaspoon turmeric powder
- 4 tablespoons oil
- 1 teaspoon mustard seeds
- 8-10 curry leaves
- 4-5 cloves
- 1 inch cinnamon stick
- 1 cup grated onion
- 1 tablespoon ginger paste
- 1 tablespoon coriander powder
- 1 tablespoon red chilli powder
- salt to taste

Method

1 Clean, wash and cut the lamb or mutton into one-inch pieces. Marinate in a mixture of yogurt, dried mango powder and turmeric powder.

2 Heat the oil in a thick-bottomed pan. Add the mustard seeds, curry leaves,

cloves and cinnamon. When the mustard seeds splutter add the grated onions and cook.

3 Add the marinated meat and ginger paste. Cook on high heat, stirring constantly.

4 Add the coriander powder, chilli powder and mango. Stir and cook for half a minute. Add two cups of water and bring to a boil. Cover the pan and simmer till the meat pieces is tender.

5 Season with salt and again cook on low heat till the gravy thickens.

6 Serve hot with the bread of your choice.

CHUTNEY FISH

Ingredients

- 600 grams *bekti* fillets, cut into 1½-inch pieces
- ½ medium bunch (175 grams) fresh spinach, chopped
- ½ cup fresh mint, chopped
- ½ cup fresh coriander, chopped
- 4 green chillies, chopped finely
- 1 small unripe green mango, chopped
- 2 tablespoons lemon juice
- salt to taste
- 6 tablespoons oil
- 1 large onion, chopped finely
- 1 inch ginger, chopped finely
- 4-5 garlic cloves, chopped finely
- 2 tablespoons coriander powder
- 1 teaspoon cumin powder
- 2 tablespoons fresh cream

Method

1 Apply the lemon juice and salt to the fish pieces and keep aside.

2 Grind the fresh mint, fresh coriander, green chillies and green mango to a fine paste, adding a little water.

3 Heat four tablespoons oil and shallow-fry the fish pieces for two to three minutes, turning them gently, to a light brown colour. Drain on absorbent paper and set aside.

4 Heat the remaining oil in a pan, add the onion and sauté for two to three minutes on medium heat or until translucent. Add the ginger and garlic and stir-fry briefly.

5 Add the coriander and cumin powders and stir well. Add the spinach and cook for two minutes on medium heat, stirring continuously.

6 Stir in the green paste, one cup water and salt to taste and bring to a boil. Reduce heat and simmer for two to three minutes, stirring occasionally.

7 Gently slide in the fish pieces, stir gently and simmer for two minutes more.

8 Stir in the fresh cream and serve hot.

KAIRI MURGH

Ingredients

- 1 whole (1 kilogram) chicken, cut into 1½-inch pieces
- 2 medium unripe green mangoes
- ½ tablespoon ginger paste
- ½ tablespoon garlic paste
- salt to taste
- 2 teaspoons *garam masala* powder
- ½ tablespoon green chilli paste
- 4-5 cloves
- 3 tablespoons oil
- 2 medium onions, finely sliced
- ¼ teaspoon turmeric powder
- 1½ teaspoons red chilli powder
- 2 teaspoons coriander powder
- 2 tablespoons chopped fresh coriander

Method

1 Peel and cut the green mangoes into small pieces. Purée half the pieces.

2 In a bowl, mix the chicken with half the ginger paste, half the garlic paste, salt, half the *garam masala* powder and half the green chilli paste and puréed mango. Marinate for about an hour, preferably in a refrigerator.

3 Place a piece of coal over a gas flame till red hot. Put it into a *katori* and place the *katori* in the bowl with the marinated chicken. Place a few cloves over the coal and pour one tablespoon of oil over. Immediately cover the bowl with a lid and leave to stand for a few minutes.

4 Heat the remaining oil in a *kadai*; add the onions and sauté till translucent. Add the remaining ginger paste, garlic paste and green chilli paste and sauté for two minutes.

5 Add the marinated chicken, turmeric powder, chilli powder, coriander powder, remaining *garam masala* powder and chopped mangoes. Stir well so that the *masala* coats the chicken.

6 Cook on high heat for a few minutes. Add the fresh coriander and a little water, cover and cook till done. Serve hot.

MANGO AND SHRIMP STIR-FRY

Ingredients

2 medium ripe mangoes, cut into ½-inch cubes

1 ½ cups shrimps, shelled and deveined

salt to taste

1 tablespoon lemon juice

1 ½ tablespoons soy sauce

1 tablespoon cornflour

1 dried red chilli, crushed

2 tablespoons sesame oil

4-6 garlic cloves, crushed

1½ inch ginger, grated

2 medium onions, cut into cubes

1 medium red capsicum, cut into strips

Method

1 Add the salt, lemon juice, half tablespoon of soy sauce and cornflour to the shrimps and mix. Add half of the crushed red chilli and mix.

2 Heat the sesame oil in a wok. Add the garlic and ginger and sauté on high heat. Add the onions and capsicum and continue to sauté.

3 Add the remaining soy sauce and a little water. Stir and cook on high heat. Add the marinated shrimps and toss.

4 Add a little water and cook for two minutes. Adjust the salt and turn off the heat.

5 Add the mango cubes and mix. Garnish with the remaining crushed red chilli and serve immediately.

AAMRAS KE MALAI ALOO

Ingredients

- ⅓ cup ripe mango pulp
- 20-25 baby potatoes
- 3 tablespoons oil + for deep-frying
- 1 teaspoon watermelon seeds
- 1 teaspoon musk melon seeds
- ¼ inch ginger
- 2 garlic cloves
- a few saffron threads
- 2 tablespoons fresh cream
- 1 teaspoon caraway seeds + ¼ teaspoon, roasted and powdered
- 3-4 green cardamoms
- 3-4 cloves
- 2 green chillies, slit
- 2 large onions, ground to a paste
- ¾ cup yogurt, whisked
- ¼ teaspoon turmeric powder
- ½ teaspoon red chilli powder
- salt to taste
- 1 teaspoon *garam masala* powder
- 6-8 peppercorns, roasted and powdered
- 2 green cardamoms, roasted and powdered

2 cloves, roasted and powdered

1 teaspoon lemon juice

Method

1 Wash and scrub the potatoes under running water. Prick them with a fork.

2 Heat sufficient oil in a *kadai* and deep-fry them with the skin till golden. Drain on absorbent paper and set aside.

3 Lightly roast the watermelon and musk melon seeds and grind to a paste using a little water. Pound the ginger and garlic to a paste with a mortar and pestle. Soak the saffron in fresh cream and set aside.

4 Heat three tablespoons of oil in a pan; add one teaspoon caraway seeds, green cardamoms and cloves. When they change colour, add the green chillies and onion paste and sauté for three to four minutes or till it turns golden brown.

5 Add the ginger-garlic paste and sauté for two minutes. Add the whisked yogurt, the melon seeds paste, turmeric powder, chilli powder and stir-fry till the oil rises to the surface. Add half a cup of water and mix well.

6 Bring the mixture to a boil. Add the mango pulp, fried potatoes and salt. Stir well.

7 Add the *garam masala* powder and the saffron-flavoured cream to the gravy and simmer for a couple of minutes. Adjust the seasoning.

8 Add the roasted and powdered caraway seeds, peppercorns, green cardamoms, cloves and lemon juice and stir. Serve hot with *paranthe*.

AAMRAS KI KADHI

Ingredients

1 cup unripe green mango pulp
1 cup ripe mango pulp
3 tablespoons gram flour
salt to taste
1 cup buttermilk
1 tablespoon oil
a pinch of asafoetida
½ teaspoon mustard seeds
¼ teaspoon fenugreek seeds
6-8 curry leaves
2 green chillies, slit
½ cup *boondi*

Method

1 In a bowl, mix together the unripe green mango pulp, ripe mango pulp, gram flour and salt till smooth. Add buttermilk and mix again.

2 Heat the oil in a deep pan. Add the asafoetida, mustard seeds, fenugreek seeds and sauté for a few seconds. Add the curry leaves and slit green chillies and sauté for two minutes.

3 Stir in the mango mixture. Add a little water, if necessary, and bring to a boil. Lower heat and simmer for ten to fifteen minutes.

4 Adjust the consistency by adding two cups of water. Add the *boondi* and simmer for five more minutes. Serve hot.

KAIRICHI AMTI

Ingredients

1 medium unripe green mango, peeled and cut into 1-inch cubes

½ cup grated coconut

5 Kashmiri red chillies

1 tablespoon coriander seeds

4 black peppercorns

1 tablespoon coconut oil

1 teaspoon mustard seeds

a pinch asafoetida

¼ teaspoon turmeric powder

salt to taste

1 tablespoon grated jaggery

1 cup coconut milk

½ cup chopped fresh coriander

Method

1 Grind the grated coconut, red chillies, coriander seeds and peppercorns with half a cup of water to a fine paste.

2 Heat the coconut oil in a pan. Add the mustard seeds. When they splutter,

add the asafoetida, turmeric powder and mango cubes and sauté.

3 Add the salt, jaggery and one-and-a-half cups of water and bring to a boil.

4 Add the ground paste to the mango mixture and cook till the mango is almost done. Mash lightly with a spoon.

5 Stir in the coconut milk and bring to a boil. Take off the heat immediately or the coconut milk will curdle.

6 Serve immediately, garnished with fresh coriander.

RAS NO FAJETO

Ingredients

- ½ cup ripe mango pulp
- 2¼ tablespoons gram flour
- ¼ teaspoon turmeric powder
- salt to taste
- 2¼ cups sour buttermilk
- 1½ tablespoons oil
- a pinch of asafoetida
- ½ teaspoon cumin seeds
- 6 curry leaves
- 2 green chillies, chopped
- ¾ tablespoon jaggery

Method

1. In a bowl, combine the mango pulp with the gram flour, turmeric powder and salt and whisk till smooth. Add the buttermilk and mix well.
2. Heat the oil in a pan; add asafoetida, cumin seeds, curry leaves and green chillies and sauté for one minute. Add the mango mixture and jaggery and mix again.
3. Add enough water to get the desired consistency.
4. Bring the mixture to a boil, lower the heat and simmer for five minutes.
5. Serve hot with steamed rice or *roti*.

AMBE BHAAT

Ingredients

- 1½ medium ripe mangoes, peeled and cut into 1-inch cubes
- 1 cup Basmati rice, soaked
- ⅓ cup mango purée
- ¾ cup milk
- 2¾ tablespoons sugar
- 2 tablespoons ghee
- 1 inch cinnamon
- 2 green cardamoms
- 2 cloves
- 6 almonds, roughly chopped
- 8 cashew nuts, roughly chopped

Method

1 Combine the mango purée, milk, sugar and three-fourth cup of water and stir till the sugar dissolves.

2 Heat the ghee in a thick-bottomed pan; add the cinnamon, cardamoms and cloves, and sauté till fragrant.

3 Drain the rice and add to the pan; sauté for one minute. Add the mango mixture and bring to a boil. Lower heat, cover and simmer till the rice is half-cooked.

4 Stir in the mango cubes and nuts. Cover and cook over low heat for another ten to fifteen minutes, or till the rice is done. Serve hot.

METHAMBA

Mango and fenugreek seed pickle

Ingredients

- 3-4 medium unripe green mangoes
- 1 teaspoon fenugreek seeds
- 2¼ cups grated jaggery
- salt to taste
- 5-6 dried red chillies
- 6-8 cloves
- 2 one-inch cinnamon sticks
- 1 cup oil
- 1 teaspoon mustard seeds
- ¼ teaspoon asafoetida

Method

1 Wash and wipe the mangoes dry. Peel and cut them into halves. Remove the seeds and cut into one-inch pieces.

2 Apply salt and set aside for twenty-four hours. Wash the mango pieces and wipe them completely dry.

3 Grind the cloves and cinnamon to a coarse powder.

4 Heat the oil in a pan, add the mustard seeds and when it starts spluttering, add the asafoetida, fenugreek seeds and dried chillies. Stir-fry briefly.

5 Add the mango pieces and jaggery. Cook on medium heat for five to six minutes or till the jaggery completely melts and coats the mango pieces.

6 Remove from heat and sprinkle the coarsely ground cloves and cinnamon powder.

7 Mix thoroughly and store the pickle in a sterilised airtight glass bottle.

AAM KA ACHAAR

Ingredients

- 500 grams unripe green mangoes
- 2½ tablespoons fennel seeds
- 1 tablespoon fenugreek seeds
- 2 teaspoons onion seeds
- 2½ teaspoons turmeric powder
- 2 tablespoons red chilli powder
- 2 teaspoons split mustard seeds
- 3½ teaspoons salt
- ¼ cup chickpeas
- 1 cup mustard oil

Method

1 Wash and wipe the mangoes dry. Peel, halve, remove the seeds and cut into half-inch cubes.

2 Grind the fennels seeds and fenugreek seeds separately to a coarse powder.

3 Place the mango cubes in a bowl; add the fennel and fenugreek seed powders, onion seeds, turmeric powder, chilli powder, mustard seeds, salt and chickpeas. Mix well.

4 Heat mustard oil in a pan to smoking point remove from heat and let the oil cool completely.

5 Add the cooled oil to the mango and mix well so that all the pieces are coated with the oil.

6 Leave the pickle to stand, covered, for three days. On the fourth day transfer the pickle to a sterilised porcelain jar.

7 Cover the mouth of the jar with a piece of muslin fastened with string. Place the jar in the sun for twelve to fifteen days to mature. Remember to shake the contents at least once a day.

8 The pickle will be ready for consumption on the twelfth day and will last for one year if stored in a cool, dry place.

ANDHRA AVAKKAI

Spicy mango pickle

Ingredients

- 12 medium unripe green mangoes
- 1 cup mustard seeds
- 2 cups red chilli powder
- ¼ cup turmeric powder
- 1½ cup salt
- ¼ teaspoon asafoetida
- 4 tablespoons fenugreek seeds
- 2 cups sesame oil
- ¼ cup chickpeas (optional)

Method

1 Wash the mangoes thoroughly and wipe them completely dry with an absorbent kitchen towel.

2 Halve the mangoes with the seed and cut each half into six to eight equal sized pieces. Spread them on a mat and dry them in the sun for about two days.

3 Dry the mustard seeds in the sun and pound to a coarse powder.

4 Thoroughly mix the chilli powder, turmeric powder, salt, asafoetida, mustard powder, fenugreek seeds and oil. De-seed the sun-dried mango pieces and mix them in the pickle *masala*. Add the chickpeas and mix.

5 Transfer to a ceramic pickle jar and cover the mouth of the jar with a piece of muslin fastened witha a string. Place the jar in the sun for three days without stirring.

6 From the fourth day onwards, stir the pickle well and continue to place in the sun for seven to ten days.

7 This pickle will last for a year if stored in a cool and dry place.

CHEF'S TIP

Use only good quality seasame oil for the pickle. Freshly pounded or milled red chilli powder is recommended.

VADU MANGO

Baby mangoes in brine

Ingredients

- 500 grams baby mangoes, soaked in brine
- 100 grams mustard powder
- 60 grams Kashmiri red chilli powder
- 50 grams salt
- a large pinch asafoetida
- 5 grams acetic acid

Method

1 Combine the mustard powder, chilli powder, salt and asafoetida with a little of the brine in which the mangoes have been soaked.

2 Drain the baby mangoes and add to the *masala*.

3 Add the acetic acid and mix. Transfer the pickle into a sterilised bottle and keep in a refrigerator.

4 Serve after a week. Always store refrigerated.

Note: For 500 grams of baby mangoes in brine, mix 350 grams baby mangoes with 75 grams of sea salt and 75 grams of vinegar. Put the mixture in a porcelain *bharni*, cover and keep for about a week or ten days before adding the *masala*.

MANGO THOKKU

Grated unripe mango pickle

Ingredients

- 6 medium unripe green mangoes, peeled and grated
- 1 teaspoon fenugreek seeds
- 1 cup sesame oil
- ½ teaspoon asafoetida
- 1 teaspoon mustard seeds
- ½ teaspoon turmeric powder
- salt to taste
- ¼ cup red chilli powder

Method

1 Broil the fenugreek seeds in a pan till dark brown. Add one tablespoon oil and asafoetida. Cool and grind to a powder.

2 Heat the rest of the oil in a pan and add the mustard seeds. When they splutter add the mangoes, turmeric powder and salt.

3 Cook on medium heat, stirring continuously, until all the moisture evaporates, the mangoes get cooked and the oil begins to separate.

4 Add the chilli powder and fenugreek powder and mix well and cook for a few more minutes.

5 Cool and store in sterilised glass bottles.

CHEF'S TIP

Adjust the quantity of salt and red chilli powder as per the size and sourness of the mangoes. Select medium to large and hard mangoes. Increase the quantity of oil if you want to store the pickle for a long time.

KERI KI LAUNJEE

Ingredients

1 kilogram unripe green mangoes

3 tablespoons mustard oil

¾ teaspoon fenugreek seeds

4 teaspoons fennel seeds

½ teaspoon onion seeds

1 teaspoon coriander powder

1 teaspoon red chilli powder

½ teaspoon turmeric powder

Salt to taste

1¼ cups grated jaggery

Method

1 Peel the mangoes, cut lengthways into quarters and remove the seeds.

2 Heat the oil in a *kadai* to smoking point. Lower the heat to medium, add the fenugreek seeds and sauté till they begin to change colour.

3 Add the fennel seeds, onion seeds, coriander powder, chilli powder, turmeric powder and salt. Mix well.

4 Add the mangoes and sauté for five minutes. Add the jaggery and half a cup of water. Bring to a boil, cover the

pan and simmer, stirring occasionally, for seven or eight minutes.

5 Remove and set aside to cool. Store in sterilised bottles when completely cold.

Note: Keri ki Launjee is a typical pickle from Rajasthan. There are three kinds of cuisine in Rajasthan – Marwari vegetarian, Jain vegetarian which is devoid of garlic and onion, and Rajput non-vegetarian and vegetarian.

GOR KERI

Ingredients

1 kilogram unripe green mangoes, peeled and cut into ½-inch cubes

6 teaspoons salt

1 teaspoon turmeric powder

1 kilogram grated jaggery

200 grams Pickle Masala (page 94)

1 tablespoon fennel seeds

Method

1 Add the salt and one teaspoon turmeric powder to the mango cubes in a large glass bowl and mix well. Cover and set aside for five to six hours. During this time the mango cubes will release water.

2 Drain the mango cubes, spread them on a large plate and dry in the sun for about six hours.

3 Place the dried mango cubes in a large glass bowl. Add the jaggery, pickle *masala* and fennel seeds and mix well.

Cover and set aside for six to eight days stirring twice daily till all the jaggery has melted.

4 Store in sterilised airtight glass or porcelain jars.

MANGO CHUTNEY

Ingredients

- 2 medium unripe green mangoes
- 1 cup fresh mint, chopped
- 2 cups fresh coriander, chopped
- 3 green chillies, chopped
- ¼ cup yogurt
- salt to taste
- 1 teaspoon sugar
- 1 teaspoon red chilli powder

Method

1. Roast the mangoes in their skins over a low gas flame. Set aside to cool.
2. Remove the skin and cut the mangoes into small pieces.
3. Mix the fresh mint and coriander, green chillies and mangoes.
4. Mix in the yogurt, salt, sugar and chilli powder.
5. Check the seasoning and store in a refrigerator till required.

SWEET MANGO CHUTNEY

Ingredients

900 grams mango, slightly under ripe, peeled and thinly sliced

900 grams sugar

4-5 garlic cloves, chopped

1 ½ inch ginger, chopped

1 teaspoon red chilli powder

1 teaspoon *garam masala* powder

2 tablespoons vinegar

Salt to taste

Method

1 Heat the mango slices in a pan with very little water till soft. Add the sugar and mix well.

2 Tie the garlic, ginger, chilli powder and *garam masala* powder loosely in a piece of muslin to make a bag (*potli*) and place in the pan.

3 Mix well and cook, on medium heat, till it reaches the consistency of a jam.Add the vinegar, salt and cook for five minutes.

4 Remove the spice bag (*potli*), cool and store the chutney in a sterilised glass bottle. Check the seasoning and store in a refrigerator till required.

Note: Unripe green mangoes can also be used to prepare the chutney.

CHEF'S TIP

To sterilise the bottle, rinse with boiling water and dry. Alternatively, you can heat the bottles in boiling water bath on medium heat for fifteen minutes, dry and use them.

CHHUNDA

Ingredients

- 2 kilograms unripe green mangoes
- 4 tablespoons salt
- ½ teaspoon turmeric powder
- 2 kg sugar
- 2-3 tablespoons red chilli powder
- 2 teaspoons cumin powder

Method

1 Wash, dry, peel and grate the mangoes.

2 Add the salt and turmeric powder to the grated mangoes. Mix well and set aside in a stainless steel pan for half an hour. Add the sugar and mix well.

3 Cook the grated mango and sugar in a thick-bottomed pan on low heat, stirring the mixture constantly.

4 Cook for about thirty to forty minutes or until the water evaporates and a one-string sugar syrup is formed. Remove from heat and let it cool.

5 When cooled, add the chilli powder and cumin powder and mix well.

6 Store in a dry, clean, sterilised glass jar with a tight lid.

CHEF'S TIP

Instead of cooking it on direct heat, chhunda can be cooked using solar energy. In a bowl, mix the sugar and mango. Cover the mouth of the bowl with a piece of muslin fastened with a string and leave it in the sun till the sugar melts to a one-string syrup consistency. Add chilli powder and cumin powder and keep it again in the sun for a day or two. Remember to stir it everyday and bring it back into the house at sunset. This quantity of chhunda will last a family of four more than a year.

MANGO AND PAPAYA JAM

Ingredients

- 2 cups (500 grams) mango pulp
- 1 medium (500 grams) papaya, peeled, cut and puréed
- 4½ cups (1 kilogram) sugar
- 6 tablespoons lemon juice

Method

1 Place the mango pulp and papaya purée in a wide pan and cook for three to four minutes.

2 Add the sugar and cook till the sugar dissolves. Add the lemon juice and cook till the mixture thickens.

3 To check if the jam is cooked and ready to be bottled, take a spoonful of the boiling jam on a plate and allow it to cool. If it sets on cooling and the water does not separate, the jam is ready to be bottled. If the water separates, continue to cook till the jam is ready.

4 Pour the jam while still hot into sterilised bottles. Let it cool completely and then seal with tight fitting lid and store.

MANGO AND COCONUT ICE CREAM

Ingredients

- 2 medium ripe mangoes
- 1 cup coconut milk
- 2 teaspoons lemon juice
- 1 cup milk
- 3 tablespoons cornflour
- ½ cup sugar
- ¼ teaspoon salt
- 2 tablespoons grated coconut
- 2 egg whites
- ½ cup fresh cream

Method

1 Peel the mangoes and make a purée of the pulp with the lemon juice. Set aside.

2 Mix together the coconut milk and half the milk in a sauce pan.

3 Mix the cornflour in the remaining milk and add sugar and salt. Add to the coconut milk mixture and cook over low heat, stirring constantly, until a thick custard is formed.

4 Add the grated coconut. Mix and set aside to cool.

5 Add the mango purée and mix well. Pour into a bowl with a lid and place in a freezer until half frozen.

6 Beat the egg whites until soft peaks are formed. Beat the cream.

7 Transfer the mango mixture to another bowl. Add the beaten egg whites and mix until smooth. Fold in the beaten cream and mix well.

8 Freeze the mixture for three hours. Remove from the freezer and beat again till smooth.

9 Return to the freezer until well-frozen.

AMBA RASAYAN

Mango coconut delight

Ingredients

- 4-5 medium ripe mangoes, cubed
- 3 cups coconut milk
- ½ cup grated jaggery
- ¼ teaspoon green cardamom powder

Method

1 In a large bowl, combine the jaggery and coconut milk and stir till the jaggery dissolves.

2 Add the mangoes and cardamom powder and stir to mix well. Serve chilled.

CHEF'S TIP

You can also use ripe bananas or musk melon to make *rasayan*.

MANGO WONTONS

Ingredients

1 cup tinned mango pulp

3 tablespoons cornflour

vanilla ice cream

Wonton Wrappers

2 cups refined flour

oil for deep-frying

Method

1 Mix the cornflour in half a cup of water. Place the mango pulp and cornflour mixture in a wok; cook, stirring continuously, till the mixture thickens and leaves the sides of the wok. Set aside to cool.

2 For the wonton wrappers, knead the refined flour with half a cup of warm water to make a firm dough.

3 Roll the dough into a large thin square sheet, about one millimetre thick. Cut the sheet into three-inch squares.

4 Place the mango filling in the centre of each square. Fold into a triangle. Twist the two edges of the folded sides and bring them together, moistening the ends with water to seal.

5 Heat the oil in a wok and deep-fry the wontons till golden. Drain on absorbent paper. Serve hot with vanilla ice cream.

FRUITY YOGURT WITH CEREAL TOPPING

Ingredients

- 2 ripe mangoes, peeled and cubed
- 2 medium apples, cubed
- 8-10 cherries, stoned
- 1½ cups yogurt, whisked
- 2 tablespoons sugar
- 1 teaspoon raisins
- 3-4 cashew nuts, chopped
- 3 tablespoons muesli, toasted

Method

1. Combine the mangoes, apples and cherries and refrigerate until ready to serve.
2. In a bowl, combine the yogurt and sugar and whisk until sugar dissolves completely.
3. Just before serving, mix in the chilled fruit, raisins and cashew nuts.
4. Spoon into individual bowls; sprinkle toasted muesli over and serve at once.

MANGO ZABAGLIONE

Ingredients

- 2 ripe mangoes
- 1 cup mango purée
- 2 egg yolks
- ¼ cup caster sugar
- 1 cup cream
- 4 tablespoons brown sugar

Method

1 Preheat the oven to 220°C/425°F/Gas Mark 7. Peel and cut the mangoes into one-inch cubes.

2 Place the mango cubes in four small individual heatproof bowls or ramekins.

3 In a heatproof bowl, mix together two egg yolks, the caster sugar and cream. Place the bowl over a pan of simmering water and cook, stirring continuously, till the mixture reaches the consistency of thick custard.

4 Add the mango purée to the custard and pass it through a sieve.

5 Pour the mango custard over the mango cubes and sprinkle brown sugar over the top. Place the bowls on a baking tray and bake for fifteen minutes. Serve hot or cold.

SINGAPOREAN MANGO JELLY

Ingredients

- 200 grams mango pulp, puréed
- 1 large mango, finely chopped
- 6 teaspoons gelatine, softened in warm water
- 150 grams sugar
- 200 ml coconut milk
- 6 tablespoons milk powder
- pomegranate kernels, for garnishing

Method

1. Combine five cups of water and sugar in a pan and cook over low heat until the sugar dissolves.

2. Add the gelatine and continue cooking until completely dissolved in the sugar syrup.

3. Remove from heat and add the coconut milk, milk powder and mango pulp and mix until well blended.

4. Add the mango and pour into individual moulds and place in a refrigerator till set.

5. Garnish with the pomegranate kernels and serve.

MANGO BHAPA DOI WITH CITRUS FRUIT

Ingredients

½ cup mango pulp

1 tin (400 grams) condensed milk

1 cup thick yogurt, whisked

½ cup milk

A few peeled orange segments

A few peeled sweet lime segments

A few pomegranate kernels

A small sprig of fresh mint

Method

1 Pour the condensed milk into a bowl. Add the yogurt, mango pulp and milk and mix well. Transfer the mixture into a heatproof container. Cover the container with aluminium foil. Heat sufficient water in a steamer and place the container in the steamer. Cover the steamer and steam for twenty to twenty-five minutes.

2 Cool and place in a refrigerator to set. Unmould onto a serving plate. Arrange the orange and sweet lime segments in a decorative pattern all around.

3 Top with a few pomegranate kernels. Place a small sprig of mint leaves on top and serve chilled.

MANGO CHEESECAKE

Ingredients

Crust

- 8-10 bran or digestive biscuits
- 4 tablespoons butter

Filling

- 2 cups mango pulp
- ½ teaspoon mango essence
- 2 cups cottage cheese
- 1 cup milk
- ½ cup condensed milk
- 1 tablespoon cornflour
- 1 tablespoon gelatine
- 1½ cups yogurt, drained
- ½ cup sugar, powdered

Topping

- 1 tablespoon mango jelly crystals
- 1 ripe mango, peeled and sliced

Method

1 Crush the biscuits to a coarse powder and place in a bowl. Rub in the butter with your fingertips. Press the mixture on to the base of a springform tin lined with greaseproof paper. Place in a refrigerator to set.

2 Heat the milk in a pan and stir in the condensed milk. Make a paste with the cornflour and a little milk, and stir into the hot milk. Cook, stirring continuously, till the mixture thickens.

3 Mix the gelatine in a little water and heat in a microwave oven for thirty seconds. Remove and set aside.

4 Place the drained yogurt into a bowl. Add the cottage cheese and whisk well. Stir in the mango pulp, mango essence and the milk mixture.

5 Add the powdered sugar and mix well with a hand mixer. Add the dissolved gelatine and mix again.

6 Pour the mixture over the biscuit layer. Refrigerate for two to three hours.

7 Dissolve the mango jelly crystals in a quarter cup of water and bring to a boil. Take the pan off the heat and leave to cool.

8 Spread a layer of mango jelly over the cheesecake. Chill until the jelly sets.

9 Remove carefully from the springform tin and cut into eight wedges with a sharp knife dipped in hot water. Serve chilled with a sliced mango fan.

Note: A springform tin is a shallow, round cake tin with a removable base.

ANNEXURE

PICKLE MASALA

To make the pickle *masala*, heat ¼ cup oil till smoking point. Remove from heat and set aside to cool completely. Lightly roast separately, 100 grams each of split skinless mustard seeds, crushed fenugreek seeds and split coriander seeds. Combine together the roasted seeds, 300 grams red chilli powder, ½ teaspoon turmeric powder and 1 teaspoon asafoetida, and mix well. Add the oil and mix again. You can store this in an airtight jar to be used when required.

CHOCOLATE SAUCE

In a pan, mix together 2 cups milk and 4 tablespoons cocoa powder. Bring the mixture to a boil. Cook till it thickens. Add ½ cup sugar, and continue to cook for three to four minutes, stirring continuously. Add ¼ cup frozen butter, cut into ½-inch pieces, and stir till melted and incorporated into the sauce. Serve warm.

GLOSSARY

English	Hindi
Almonds	Badam
Apple	Saeb
Asafoetida	Hing
Banana	Kela
Brine	Namak paani
Butter	Makkhan
Butter milk	Chhaach
Capsicum, green	Hari Shimla mirch
Capsicum, red	Lal shimla mirch
Capsicum, yellow	Pili Shimla mirch
Caraway	Shahi jeera
Cardamoms, green	Chhoti elaichi
Cashew nuts	Kaju
Chicken	Murgh
Chickpeas	Kabuli chana
Chillies, dried red	Sookhi lal mirch
Chillies, fresh red	Taazi lal mirch
Chillies, green	Hari mirch
Cinnamon	Dalchini
Cloves	Laung
Coconut	Nariyal
Coriander seeds	Dhania
Coriander, fresh	Hara dhania
Cottage cheese	Paneer
Cream	Malai
Cumin seeds	Jeera
Curry leaves	Kadhi patta
Dates	Khajur
Egg	Anda
Egg, white	Ande ki safedi
Egg, yolks	Ande ki Zardi
Fennel seeds	Saunf
Fenugreek seeds	Methi dana
Flour, refined	Maida
Garlic	Lehsun
Gelatine	Sares
Ginger, dried	Sonth
Ginger, fresh	Adrak
Gram flour	Besan
Grapes	Angoor

Honey .... Shahad/madhu
Jaggery .... Gur
Lemon .... Nimbu
Lettuce .... Salad ke patte
Mango, baby .... Chhote aam
Mango, ripe................................. Aam
Mango, unripe green .... Keri
Milk... Doodh
Mint leaves, fresh .... Pudina ke pattiyan
Musk melon .... Kharbooj
Musk melon seeds........ Kharbooj magaj
Mustard seeds .... Rai
Mustard seeds, split .... Rai dal
Mutton .... Gosht
Onion.. Pyaaz
Onion seeeds .... Kalonji
Orange........................ Narangi/santara
Papaya .... Papita
Peppercorns, black .... Kali mirch
Pineapple .... Ananas
Pistachios .... Pista

Pomegranate .... Anar
Potatoes, baby .... Chhote aloo
Prawns .... Jheenga
Raisins..................................... Kishmish
Rose .... Gulab
Saffron .... Kesar
Salt, black.......................... Kala namak
Salt, rock .... Sendha namak
Salt, sea .... Samudri namak
Sesame seeds .... Til
Shallots........................... Chhote pyaaz
Shrimps .... Chhote jheenge
Spinach leaves .... Palak ke taze patte
Sugar .... Cheeni/shakkar
Sweet lime............................ Mosambi
Tamarind .... Imli
Tomatoes .... Tamatar
Turmeric powder .... Haldi
Water melon .... Tarbooj
Water melon seeds .... Tarbooj magaz
Yogurt... Dahi